Farms Feed the World

Farms Feed the World

a building block book

Lee Sullivan Hill

Carolrhoda Books, Inc./Minneapolis

For farmers all over the world who continue to work the land while houses and factories encroach ever closer.—L. S. H.

The photographs in this book are reproduced through the courtesy of: Bob Firth/Firth Photobank, front cover, pp. 1, 6, 8, 12, 19, 25; Howard Ande, pp. 2, 23, 28; Buddy Mays/ Travelstock, back cover, pp. 5, 7, 11, 13, 15, 16, 17, 18; Voscar—The Maine Photographer, pp. 9, 20; Peter Ford, pp. 10, 24; Phil Lauro, p. 14; Steven Ferry, p. 21; Paul T. McMahon, pp. 22, 27; Cheryl Walsh Bellville, p. 26; Elaine Little, p. 29.

For metric conversion, when you know the number of gallons, multiply by 3.79 to find the number of liters.

Carolrhoda Books, Inc., c/o The Lerner Publishing Group
241 First Avenue North, Minneapolis, MN 55401 U.S.A.

Library of Congress Cataloging-in-Publication Data

Hill, Lee Sullivan, 1958–
    Farms feed the world / Lee Sullivan Hill.
        p.   cm. — (A building block book)
    Includes index.
    Summary: A simple introduction to the beauty and variety of farms from a wheat field in Montana to the harvesting of seaweed from the ocean.
    ISBN 1-57505-075-7
    1. Agriculture—Juvenile literature. 2. Farms—Juvenile literature. 3. Farm life— Juvenile literature. [1. Agriculture. 2. Farms. 3. Farm life.] I. Title. II. Series: Hill, Lee Sullivan, 1958– Building block book.
    S519.H49   1997
    630—dc21   96-51015

Manufactured in the United States of America
1 2 3   4 5 6 SP 02 01 00 99 98 97

Farms are some of the most important places
on earth. Everybody needs food to eat and
clothes to wear. Farmers work hard each day
to bring us these things.

Farms can be small.
A vegetable garden and
a few chickens make up
this family farm.

Farms can be big. A vast Montana wheat field
stretches like a fuzzy blanket from one edge of
the sky to the other.

On many farms, crops are grown for people to eat. Farmers grow cranberries in soggy bogs. Do you like cranberry jelly with your turkey on Thanksgiving?

How about mashed potatoes? Potato plants
look green and leafy in the field. You can even
pick their flowers. But you can't see the potatoes.
The part you eat grows underground.

You can see bits of white on these plants.
Don't try to eat them! After harvesting, the
cotton will be made into cloth—not food. Your
T-shirt started out as wispy cotton in a field.

Your sweater may have come from a sheep's woolly coat in New Zealand. Farmers shear the sheep one by one. Then the wool is sent to a factory and spun into yarn.

Some farms raise animals so people can eat
meat. Hot dogs, ham, and bacon come from hogs.

Steaks and hamburgers come from cattle.

Farmers often grow hay for their cattle to eat.

These farms raise both plants and animals.

Some farms have ponds full of growing fish. Fish farmers raise salmon, catfish, striped bass, and trout. When the fish grow big enough to eat, the farmer harvests them. They end up in grocery stores and restaurants.

Seaweed grows in water, too. After being harvested, it gets mixed into ice cream and other foods you eat. But don't worry. You won't taste it. It is dried and ground into a fine powder first.

Millions of people eat rice as their main food.
Farmers plant rice in fields called paddies. On
small farms, families tend the crop by hand.

Corn is another important crop. Some corn gets ground into cornmeal. Some is eaten right off the cob. Shucking ears of corn is a job for the whole family on a hot summer day.

Farm work goes on no matter what the weather.
In winter, cold winds push right through a winter
coat. Animals need extra food to keep warm.

Sometimes winter seems like it will never end. Ice and snow cover the fields. But work goes on inside. Farmers pay last year's bills and plan next year's crops. They fix tools and machines.

When spring finally arrives, the smell of fresh earth fills the air. Plows turn over the dark earth row by row by row to get it ready for planting.

Spring means baby animals on many farms.
On horse farms, young colts wobble to their feet
for the very first time.

Spring leads to summer and that means no school. But on farms, it means more work. Heads up! Hay bales fly out of the baler and into the wagon.

All summer long, animals grow bigger.
Crops grow taller. Weeds grow, too. Farmers
use machines to keep the weeds away.

By fall, the crops are as tall as they can get.
They're ripe and ready for harvest. Huge machines
called harvesters gather in wide fields of wheat.

You can go to a farm at harvest time to choose your own pumpkin. You might even get a hayride while you're there.

Next time you go to the market, think about farms. That tasty pepper came from someone's vegetable farm. Your jeans came from a farmer's cotton field.

When you grow up, you could drive a tractor. You could shear wool from sheep. Or you could live by the ocean and harvest seaweed for a living.

Farms give us food. They give us clothes.
They give us the sound of a rooster crowing and
the sight of a barn in the setting sun.

Farms take care of people all over the world.

A Photo Index to the Farms in This Book

Cover This farm raises both plants and animals. Black and white cows crowd into the barnyard every day. They are Holsteins, a kind of cattle bred for milking. The average cow makes 1,600 gallons of milk a year.

Page 1 This kind of corn, often called maize, is grown as food for people or animals. People also use the many-colored ears of corn as decorations at home and at school.

Page 2 Red barns color a foggy day. Barns are important on a farm. They keep tractors, animals, and hay out of bad weather.

Page 5 This dairy farmer lives in the Cotswold Hills of England. Farmers milk their cows every twelve hours—early in the morning and at the end of the day.

Page 6 People passing by can stop in to buy eggs at this farm in Minneota, Minnesota. The windmill once pumped water for the farm from a well.

Page 7 Wheat is second only to rice in the number of people it feeds around the world.

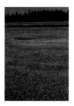

Page 8 A farmer in Eagle River, Wisconsin, has flooded his cranberry fields on purpose. The ripe cranberries float to the top and can then be gathered.

Page 9 These potato blossoms in Mapleton, Maine, look pretty. But have you ever seen a potato gone to seed? Hairy roots stick out all over. It looks like an alien! Try leaving a potato under the kitchen sink for a while and see what happens.

Page 10 Seeds are mixed in with the fluffy cotton on these plants. The cotton gin, invented by Eli Whitney in 1793, helps workers quickly sort the seeds from the cotton.

Page 11 Sheep thrive in the hilly, rocky areas near Queenstown, New Zealand. Would you believe that there are 20 times more sheep than people in New Zealand?

 **Page 12** A farmer feeds pigs in Cosmos, Minnesota. A milking barn stands in the background—the farmer also raises dairy cattle. Large hog ranches raise as many as a thousand pigs at a time. (Farms that raise lots of animals are often called ranches.)

 **Page 13** This rancher in New Mexico has oil wells on his land. They bring in extra money, which helps buy hay for his cattle.

 **Page 14** The trout raised at the Leadville Fish Hatchery in Colorado will be released in rivers so that sport fishers have more fish to catch.

 **Page 15** The seaweed harvested at Grand Manan Island in New Brunswick, Canada, is used as food. Harvesters gather the seaweed, called dulse, when the Atlantic Ocean lies at low tide.

 **Page 16** A worker in Bali, Indonesia, tends new rice shoots. A good crop depends greatly on a farmer's care. Rice feeds more people around the world than any other crop.

 **Page 17** This family in New Mexico is shucking sweet corn. Will they sell the corn at a farmers' market?

 **Page 18** A horse-drawn sled helps this rancher in Colorado bring hay to his herd. Some of the cattle have red coats and white faces. They are Herefords, a breed of cattle raised for meat.

 **Page 19** Near Wasioja, Minnesota, it can be as cold as 60 degrees below zero in winter. Nothing but ice grows at that temperature!

 **Page 20** A farmer in Aroostook County, Maine, pulls a harrow with his tractor. The harrow has metal disks on a steel rod. The disks break up clods of dirt as they roll across the field.

 **Page 21** This farm raises purebred quarter horses. Female horses, known as mares, can give birth to one or two foals each spring. The foals struggle to stand up right after they are born.

 **Page 22** Hay is really tall grass that has been cut and dried. Balers scoop up the cuttings, form them into bales, and toss them out the back of the machine. Farmers harvest hay fields several times each season. How often do you mow your lawn at home?

 **Page 23** This farmer in Illinois is cultivating his corn crop. A cultivator looks like an iron comb. Its teeth pull up weeds and loosen the soil so that rain and air will reach the roots of the plants.

 **Page 24** Fall is the end of the growing season—or is it? In some places, farmers grow winter wheat—wheat that is planted in the fall and harvested in spring.

 **Page 25** Piles of pumpkins are for sale near Victoria, Minnesota. This farm sells Christmas trees, fruits, and vegetables at other times of the year.

 **Page 26** Have you ever visited a farmers' market? Besides fruits and vegetables, you might find honey, baked treats, and handmade sweaters.

 **Page 27** Equipment makes it possible to farm more land with fewer workers. But there are still farm jobs for people all over the world. Did you know that you can go to college and study to become a farmer?

 **Page 28** A sunset in Cortland, Illinois, makes the sky glow. The farmer raises dairy cattle and grows corn and soybeans.

 **Page 29** Mother and daughter walk along the top of a wall between rice paddies in the Philippines. They are on their way to a town market to sell green peppers from their farm.